SCHIRMER'S LIBRARY OF MUSICAL CLASSICS

Vol. 2132

95 WALTZES FOR PIANO
By 16 Composers

Brahms, Chopin, Debussy, Grieg, Liszt, Ravel, Schubert, Tchaikovsky, and more

ISBN 978-1-4950-9052-3

G. SCHIRMER, Inc.

DISTRIBUTED BY

HAL•LEONARD®

7777 W. BLUEMOUND RD. P.O. BOX 13819 MILWAUKEE, WI 53213

www.musicsalesclassical.com
www.halleonard.com

CONTENTS

Waltz
in E-flat Major

Ludwig van Beethoven
WoO 84

Fine

Trio

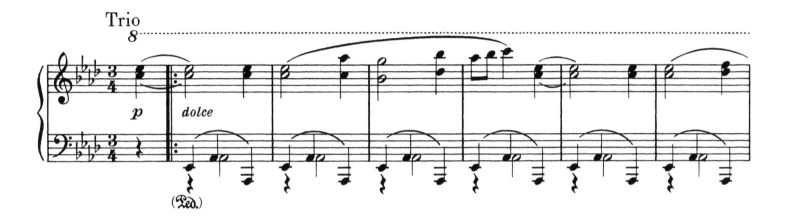

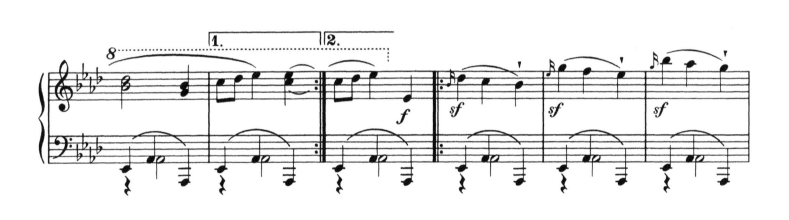

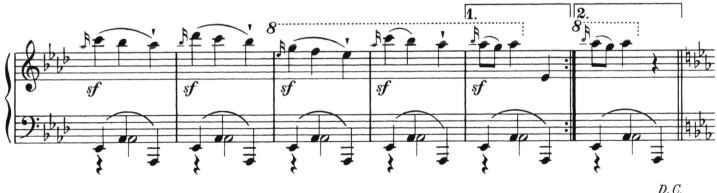

D.C.

Waltz
from *The First Term at the Piano*

Béla Bartók
Sz. 53

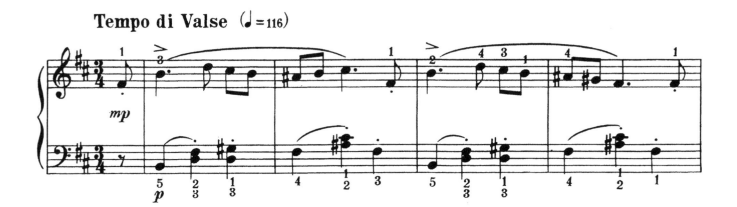

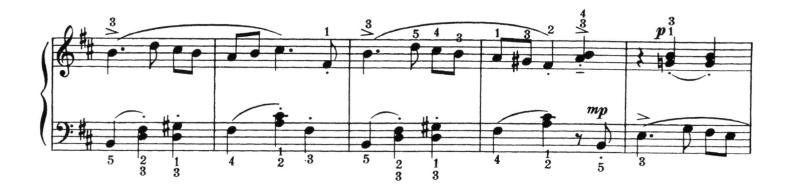

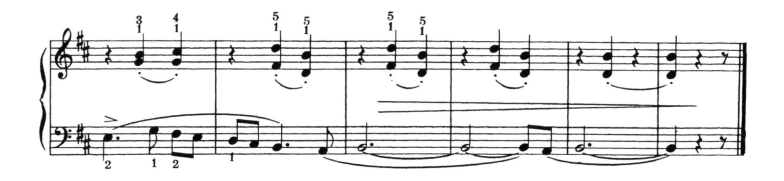

Dedicated to Dr. Eduard Hanslick

Sixteen Waltzes

Simplified Edition

Johannes Brahms
Op. 39

8

2

3

Poco sostenuto

4

appassionato

col 8va ad lib. . . . .

5 Grazioso

6 Vivace

Poco più Andante

7

8

9

10

12

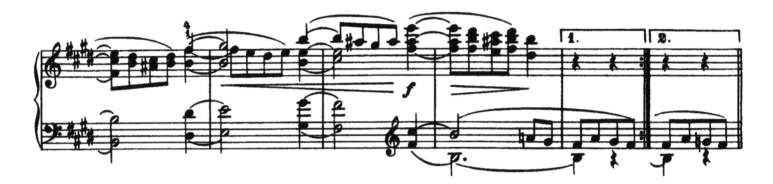

13

14

15 *p dolce*

poco cresc.

poco cresc. *p*

p dolce

16

à Laura Harsford

Grand valse brillante
in E-flat Major

Frédéric Chopin
Op. 18

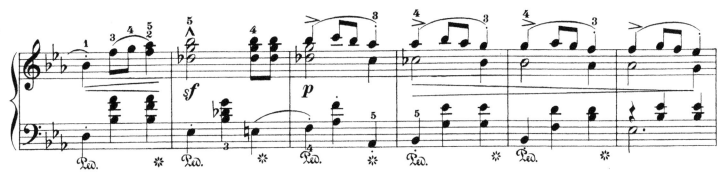

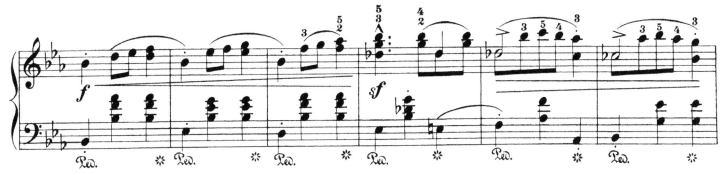

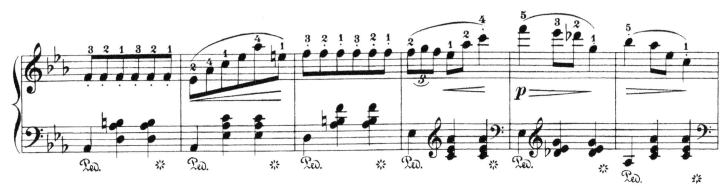

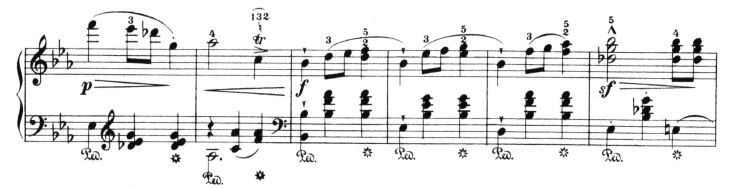

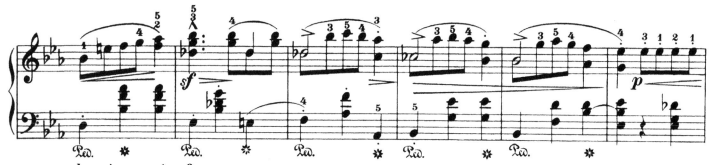

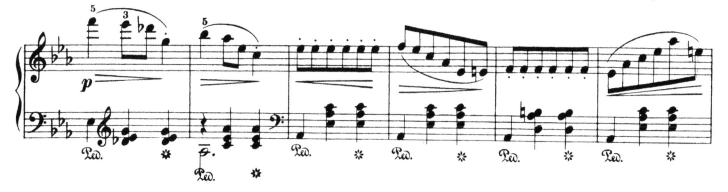

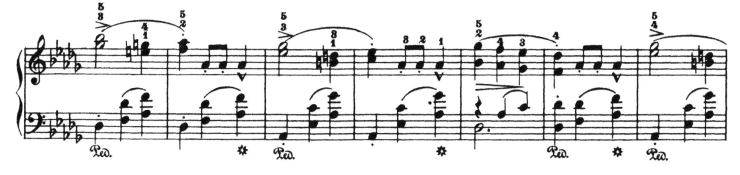

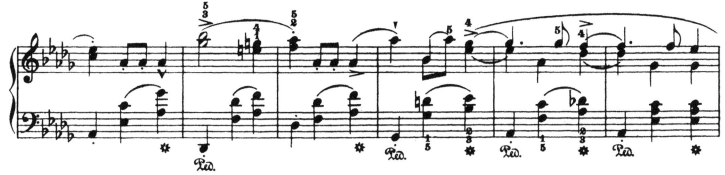

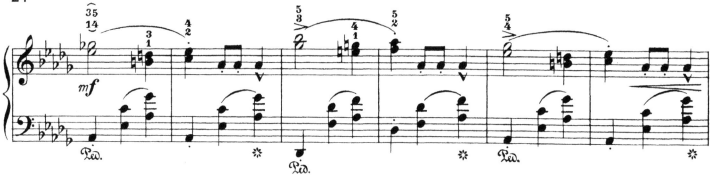

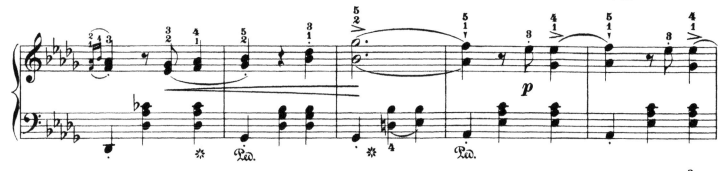

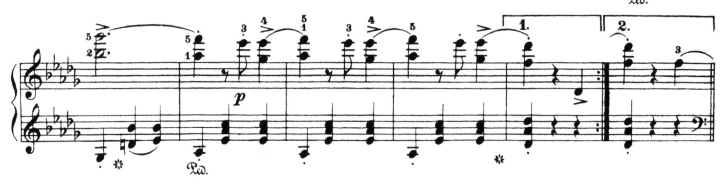

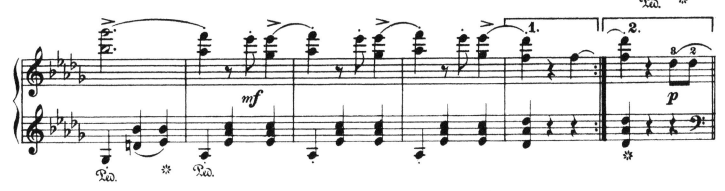

à Madame la Contesse Delphine Potocka

Waltz
in D-flat Major
"Minute"

Frédéric Chopin
Op. 64, No. 1

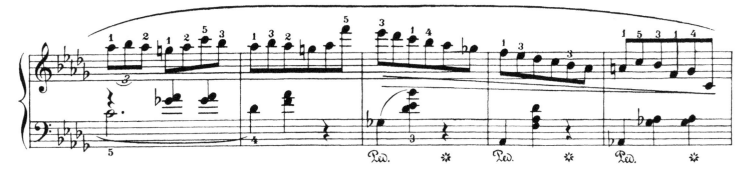

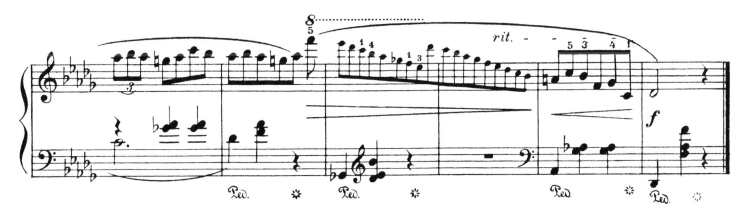

Waltz
in A-flat Major

Frédéric Chopin
Op. 69, No. 1
(Posthumous)

Waltz
in B minor

Frédéric Chopin
Op. 69, No. 2
(Posthumous)

Waltz
in F minor

Frédéric Chopin
Op. 70, No. 2
(Posthumous)

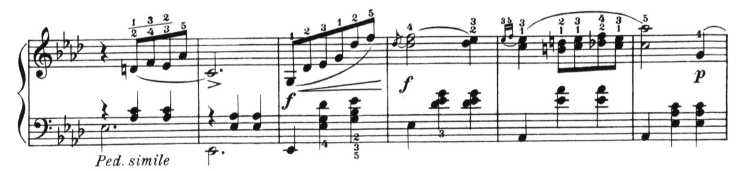

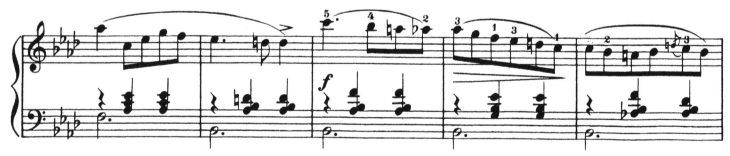

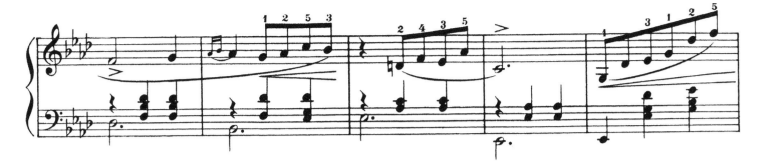

Waltz
in E Major

Frédéric Chopin
KK. IVa, No. 12

Tempo di Valse

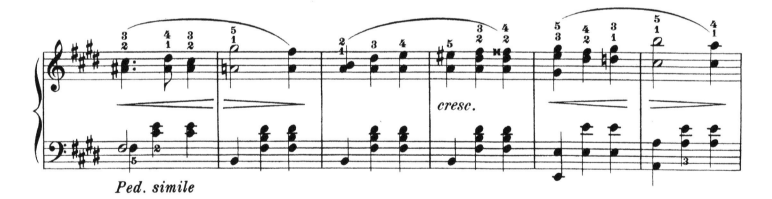

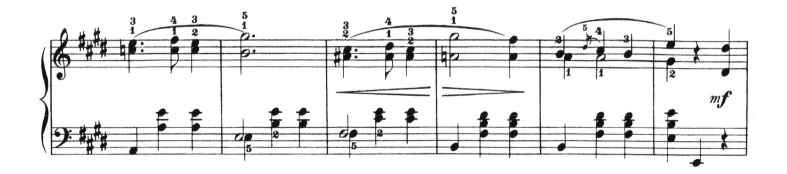

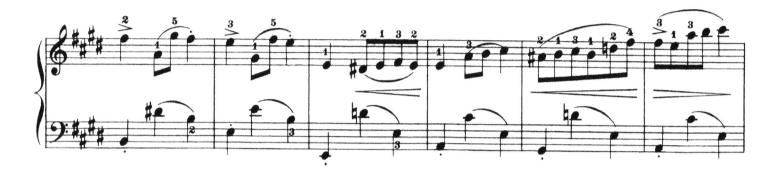

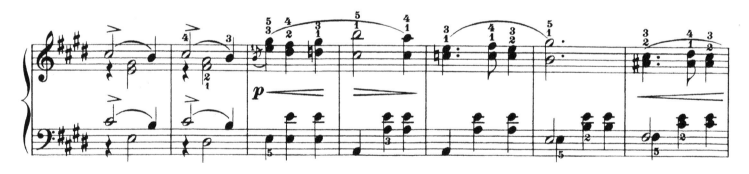

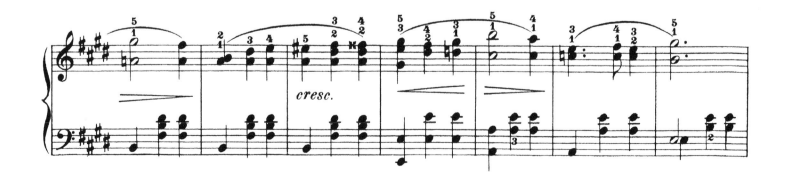

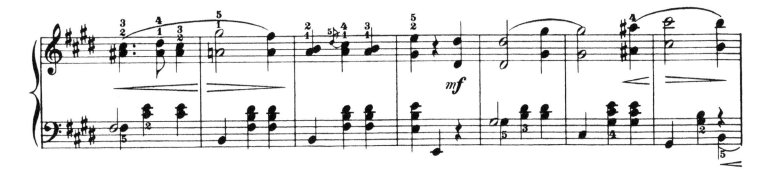

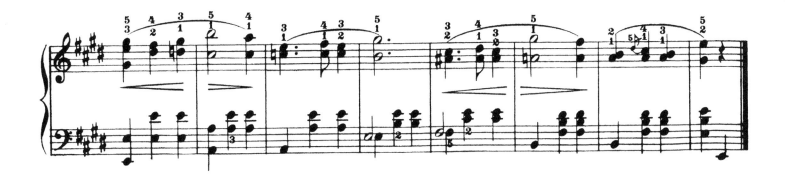

Waltz
in D-flat Major

Frédéric Chopin
Op. 70, No. 3
(Posthumous)

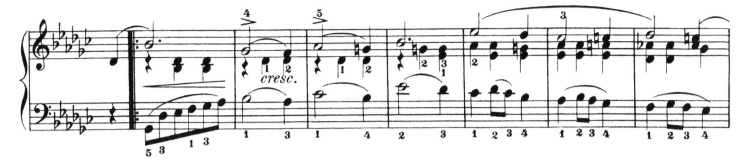

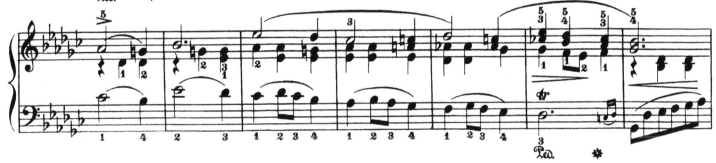

Selections from
Valses Poeticos

Enrique Granados

Nº 1

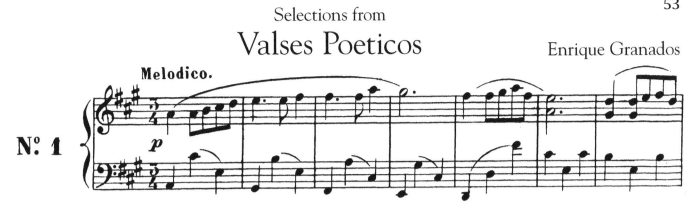

Tempo de Vals noble.

Nº 2

Tempo de Vals lento.

Nº 3

D.C. al Fine

Allegro humoristico.

N.º 4

D.C. al Fine

Allegretto (elegante)

N.º 5

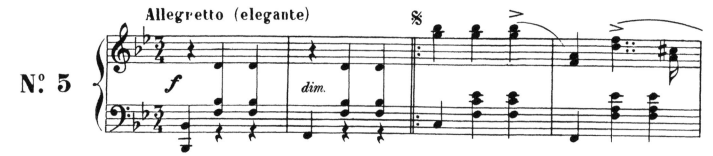

D.S. al
Fine

Valse Noble

from *Albumleaves for the Young*

Cornelius Gurlitt
Op. 101, No. 14

Moderato

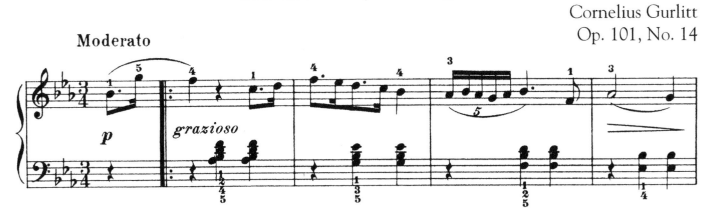

Valse romantique

Claude Debussy

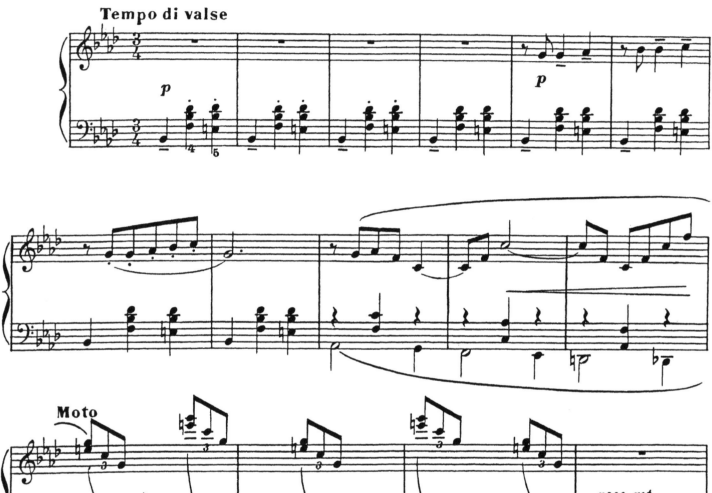

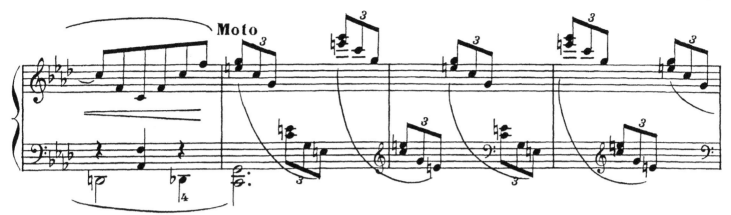

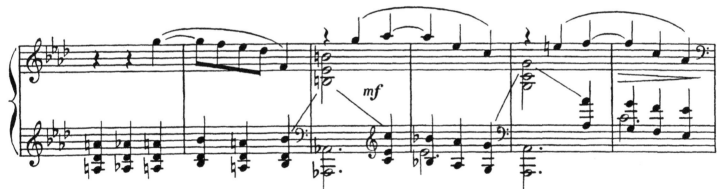

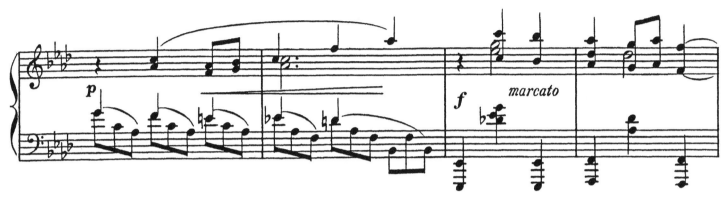

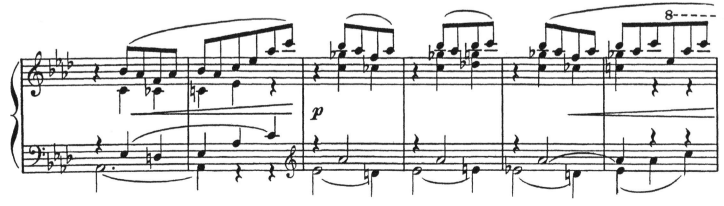

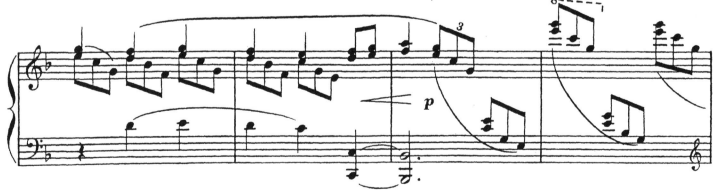

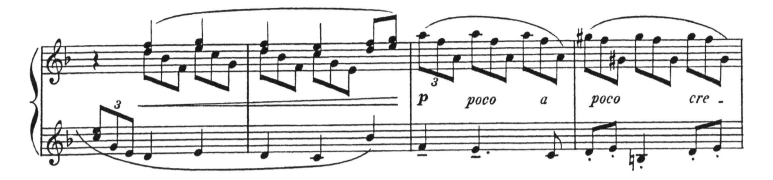

Waltz
in A Major

Antonin Dvořák
Op. 54, No. 1

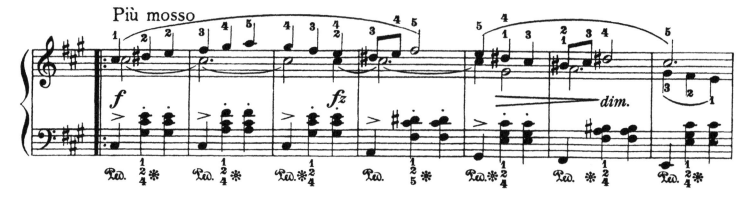

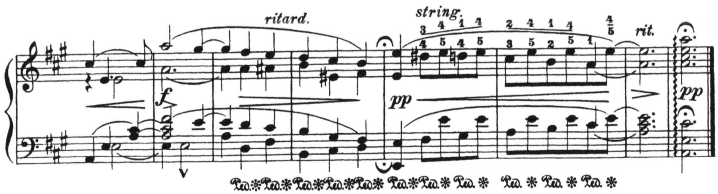

Waltz

from *Lyric Pieces*

Edvard Grieg
Op. 12, No. 2

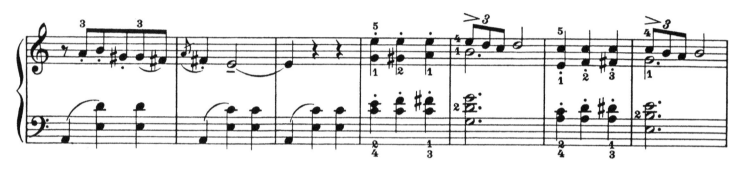

Coda

Waltz
from *Lyric Pieces*

Edvard Grieg
Op. 38, No. 7

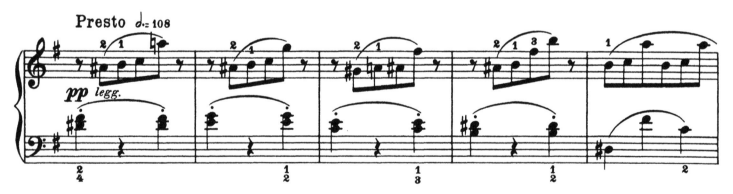

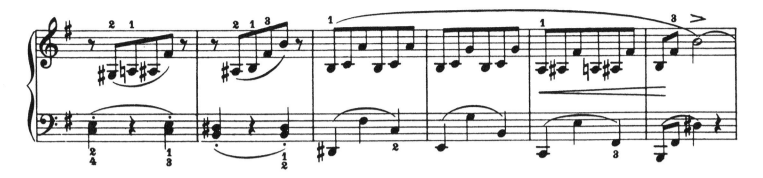

Tempo I

Valse Impromptu

from *Lyric Pieces*

Edvard Grieg
Op. 47, No. 1

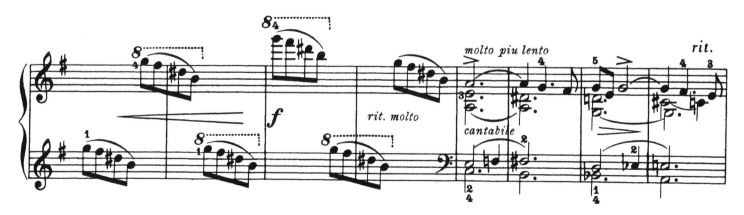

Tempo I

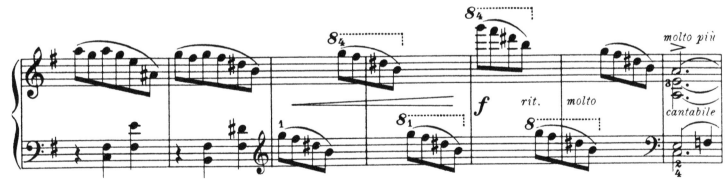

Melancholy Waltz

from *Lyric Pieces*

Edvard Grieg
Op. 68, No. 6

Tempo di Valse tranquillo

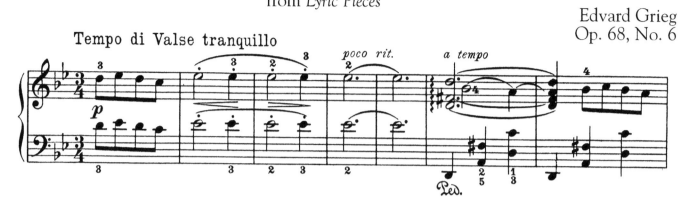

Tempo I

Tempo I
tranq.

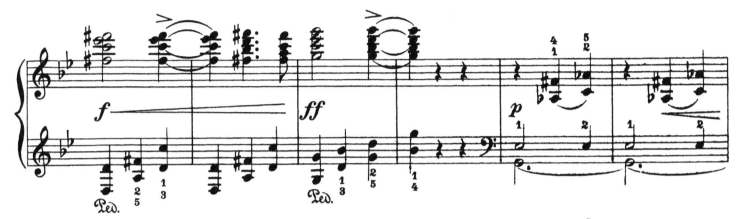

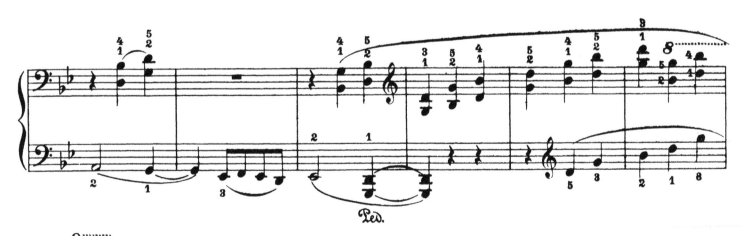

Petite Valse

from *25 Melodious Studies*

Stephen Heller
Op. 45, No. 13

Allegro scherzando.

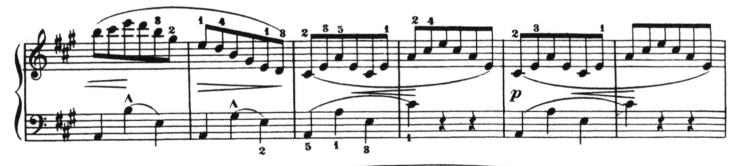

Pleasant Moments
Ragtime Waltz

Scott Joplin

Slow waltz time

poco accel.

Fine

Bethena
A Concert Waltz

Scott Joplin

Tema
Valse tempo

rit. poco a poco

Valse cantabile
a tempo

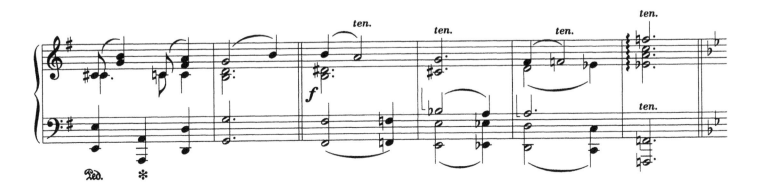

Cantabile

Cantabile

Finale

Andante

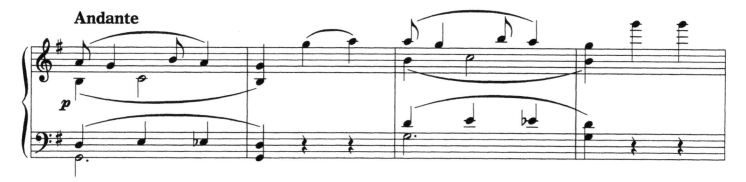

Tempo primo

Fine

Waltz
in A Major

Franz Liszt
S. 208a

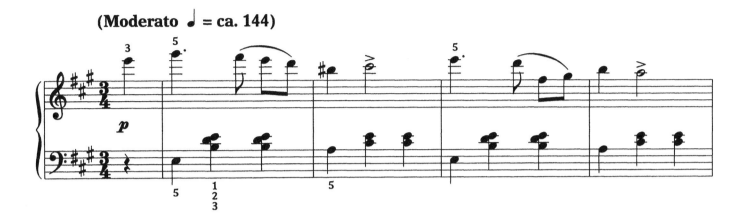

Album Leaf in Waltz Form
Simplified Transcription

Franz Liszt
S. 166

12 Valses Nobles

Franz Schubert
Op. 77
D 969

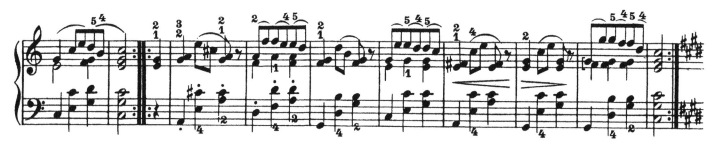

11.

12.

12 Valses Sentimentales

Franz Schubert
from Op. 50
D 779

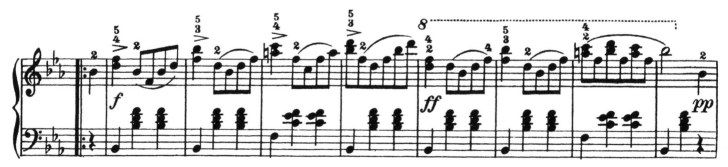

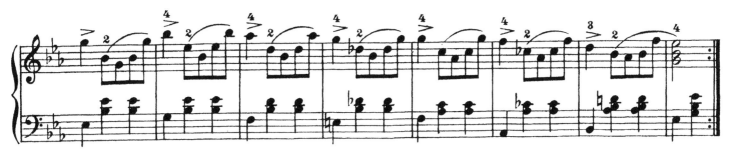

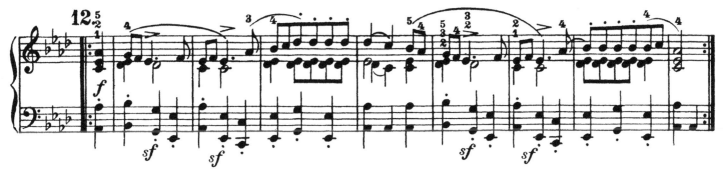

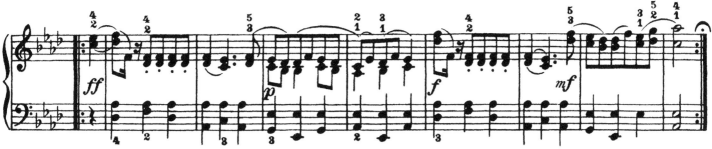

13 Last Waltzes

Franz Schubert
from Op. 50
D 779

D.C.

4.

Trio

D.C.

5.

D.C.

D.C.

D.C.

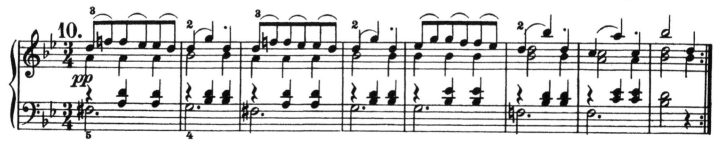

Waltz
in G Major

Franz Schubert
D 844

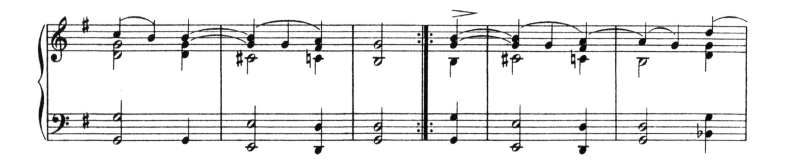

Valses nobles et sentimentales

"…the ever-renewed delight
of a useless pastime."

Maurice Ravel

(Henri de Regnier)

I

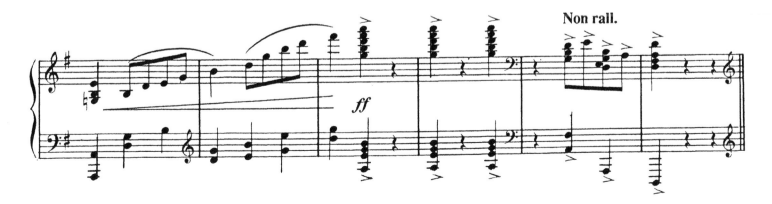

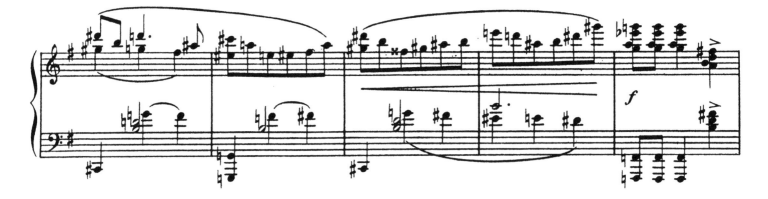

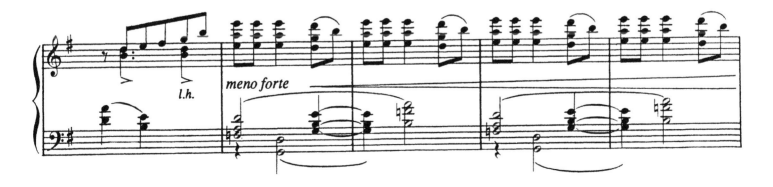

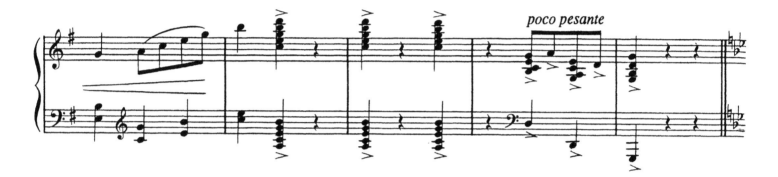

II

Lento assai—with intense expression ♩ = 104

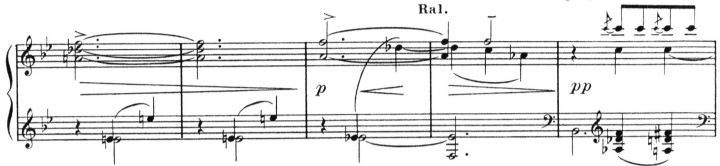

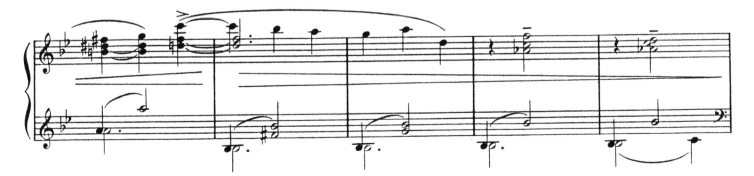

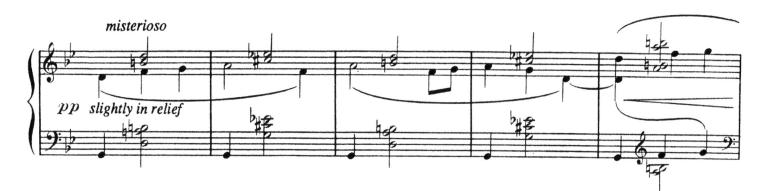

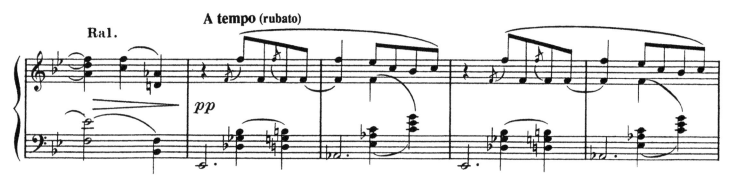

III

Moderato

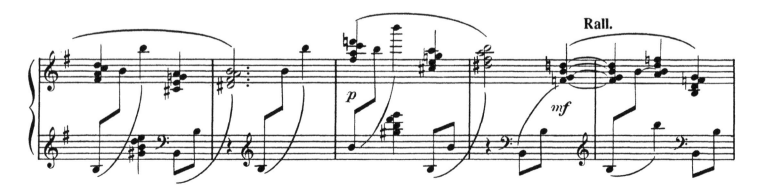

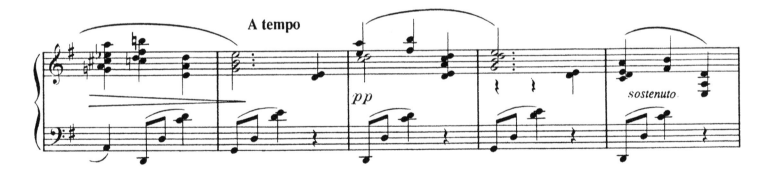

IV

Pocchissimo rall.   **A tempo**

slightly in relief

V

VI

Rallentando

A tempo

Pocchissimo rall. **A tempo**

very soft and somewhat languishing

À la manière de…Borodine
(In the style of…Borodin)
Valse

Maurice Ravel

Allegro giusto

Valse Noble

from *Carnaval*

Robert Schumann
Op. 9

Un poco maestoso ♩ = 138

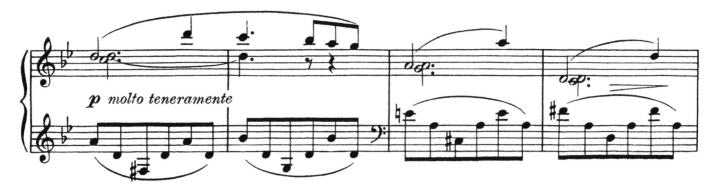

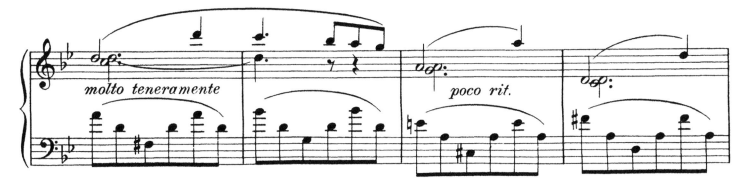

Valse Allemande

from *Carnaval*

Robert Schumann
Op. 9

Waltz in A minor
from *Album Leaves*

Robert Schumann
Op. 124, No. 4

Animato ♩. = 72

Waltz in E-flat Major

from *Album Leaves*

Robert Schumann
Op. 124, No. 10

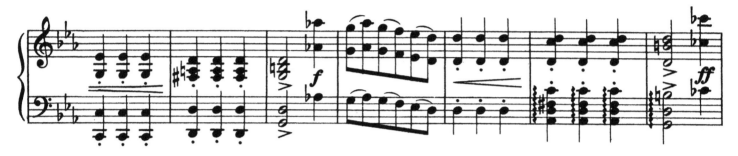

Waltz in A-flat Major

from *Album Leaves*

Robert Schumann
Op. 124, No. 15

Waltz

from *Album for the Young*

Pyotr Il'yich Tchaikovsky
Op. 39, No. 8

Waltz of the Flowers

from *The Nutcracker Suite*

Pyotr Il'yich Tchaikovsky
Op. 71A

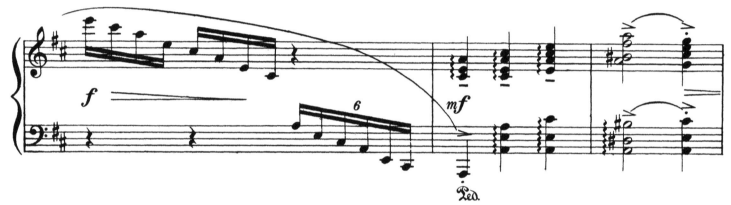

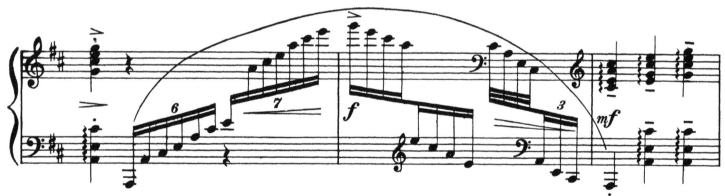

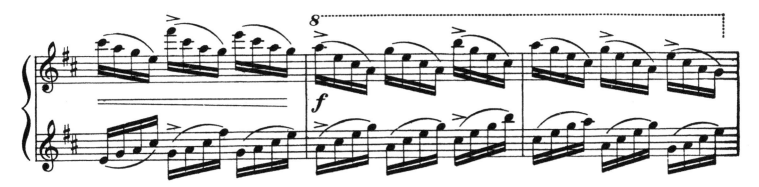

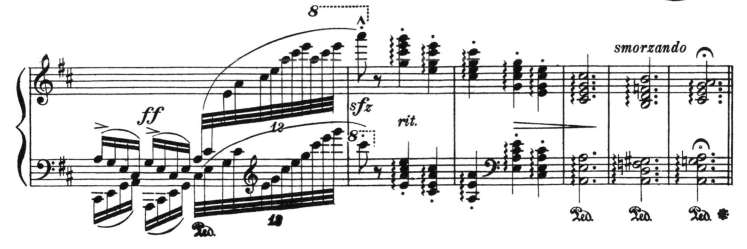

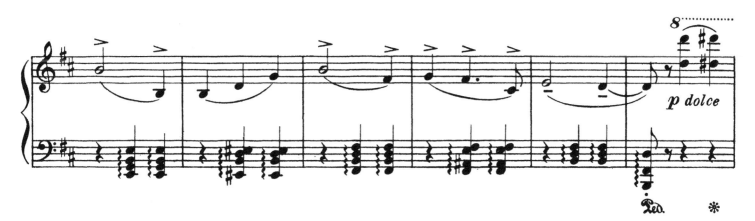

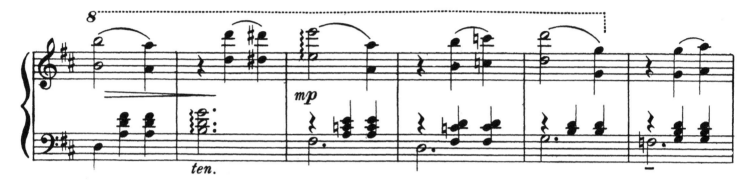

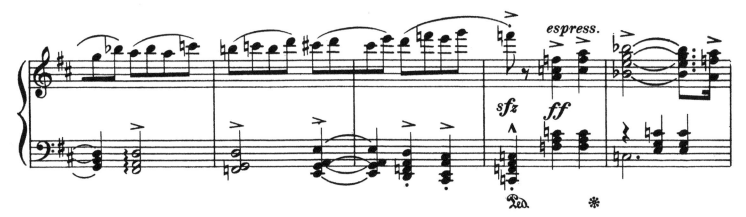

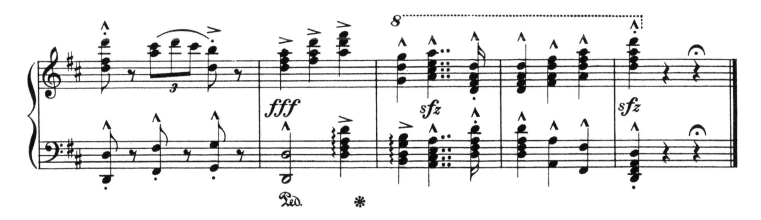